Great Events

The SPANISH ARMADA

Written and Illustrated
by Gillian Clements

W
FRANKLIN WATTS
LONDON•SYDNEY

This edition 2014

First published in 2003 by
338 Euston Road
London NW1 3BH

Franklin Watts Australia
Level 17/207 Kent Street

Copyright © 2002 Gillian Clements

The right of the author to be identified
as the author of this work has been asserted.

ISBN 978 1 4451 3160 3

Dewey Decimal Classification Number: 941.06

A CIP catalogue record for this book
is available from the British Library.

Series editor: Rachel Cooke
Historical consultant: Claire Edwards
Printed in Great Britain

Franklin Watts is a division of Hachette Children's
Books, an Hachette UK company.
www.hachette.co.uk

The SPANISH ARMADA

1588 was going to be a year of
"wonderful and extraordinary
accidents", someone predicted.
When King Philip's Grand Fleet of
ships – the Armada – sailed
towards England's shores, that
prediction came true.

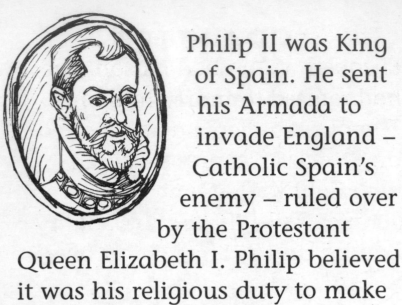

Philip II was King of Spain. He sent his Armada to invade England – Catholic Spain's enemy – ruled over by the Protestant Queen Elizabeth I. Philip believed it was his religious duty to make England Catholic again. It was his, and other Catholics, "Enterprise on England".

4

The Spanish King hated Elizabeth with good reason. She had refused to marry him once. Then her soldiers had supported the Dutch Protestants in their long fight to free their lands from Spanish rule. As a result, Spain had lost much of its power over the Low Countries.

And the Queen's privateers… "They are Elizabeth's pirates!" thundered the Spanish King. "Her sea captains sail to our Spanish towns in South America, raid our ports and ships there – and steal our gold and silver."

The Spanish had grown rich on the treasures they had found in the "New World" of America. Now, the English were, too! Sir Francis Drake had looted every Spanish galleon he had found. Spaniards called him *"El Draque"* – the Dragon.

King Philip plotted revenge. "I will build a great Armada and sink the English navy," he decided. "Then my army in the Low Countries can storm England's shores, and march on London."

King Philip was proud of his army. "Our 'Blackbeards' are the finest, and our Catholic cause is right!"

The Duke of Parma, Spain's governor in the Low Countries, thought it was time to fight, too. He wanted to stop the English helping the Dutch rebels. "God is on our side," he agreed with his king.

God is on our side.

9

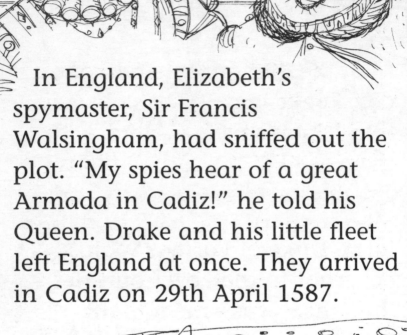

In England, Elizabeth's spymaster, Sir Francis Walsingham, had sniffed out the plot. "My spies hear of a great Armada in Cadiz!" he told his Queen. Drake and his little fleet left England at once. They arrived in Cadiz on 29th April 1587.

On the 30th, they left. In one day, Drake wrecked or stole over thirty Spanish ships – and, with them, all Philip's careful plans. Drake even took the stores and ammunition. "I have singed the King of Spain's beard!" he boasted.

But the English knew the Armada would rise again. They had to prepare.

Elizabeth appointed her cousin, Lord Howard of Effingham, Admiral of all the English fleet. Drake would command a squadron, as would two other English "sea dogs" – John Hawkins and Martin Frobisher.

Philip made the Duke of Medina Sidonia commander of the Armada. But he was no sailor. "Sir, I have not health for the sea… I soon become seasick," he wrote to his king. Secretly he feared the Armada was doomed. "Can we sink all England's ships and make it safe to invade?"

But the King stood his ground. He explained his plan to use the Duke of Parma and his soldiers from their base in Flanders in the Low Countries. "On seeing the narrow seas made safe by the Armada..." he wrote back to Medina Sidonia, "Parma will immediately send across the army in small boats."

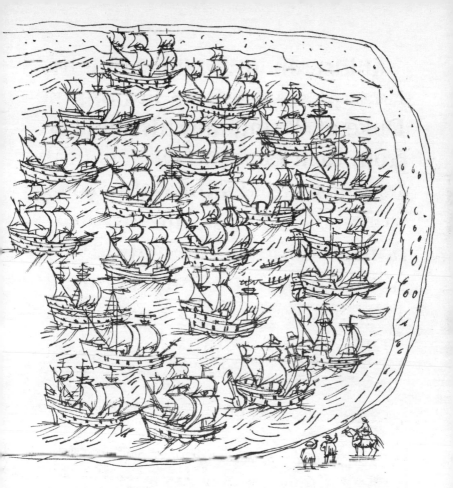

The new Armada was complete, the ships loaded and the soldiers on board. There could be no more delays. Men were already dying in the cramped and dirty ships, and others were running away.

At last, on 28th May 1588, the Armada set sail from Lisbon. Almost immediately, they hit a gale "as bad as if it were December!". Medina Sidonia had to go back to Corunna in northern Spain. The Armada did not sail again until July.

North of Philip's Armada, an English ship was sailing off the coast of Cornwall. It was 29th July. Suddenly, on the horizon, the crew saw, "nine sails of great ships... all crossed over with a red cross!"

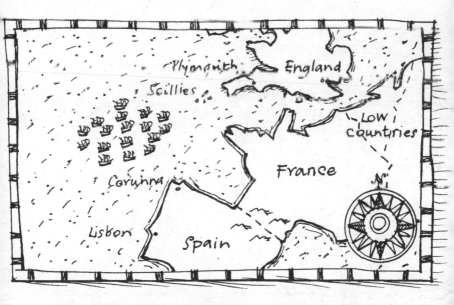

The ship rushed back to England with the news – the Armada had reached the Scillies.

The Armada moved north. It was sighted from land now, too. Drake was playing bowls on Plymouth Hoe at the time, so people said. "We can finish the game, and beat the Spaniards, too!" he joked.

Below him, England's ships lay at anchor. Over a hundred, big and small – every vessel Admiral Howard, Commander of the English fleet, could find!

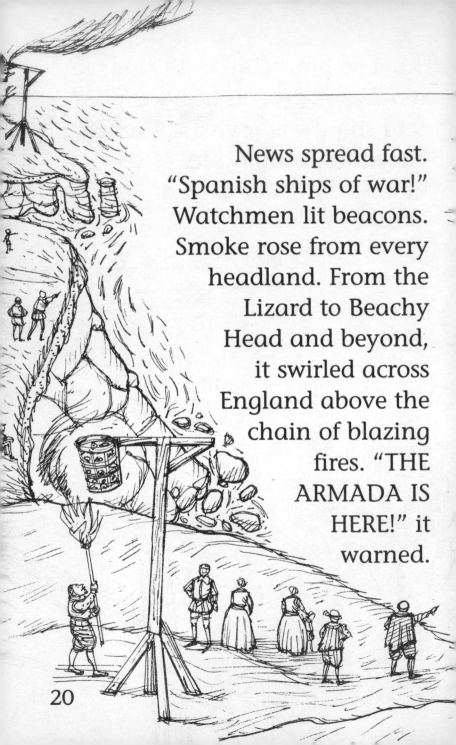

News spread fast. "Spanish ships of war!" Watchmen lit beacons. Smoke rose from every headland. From the Lizard to Beachy Head and beyond, it swirled across England above the chain of blazing fires. "THE ARMADA IS HERE!" it warned.

Medina Sidonia sent his message too, to Parma in Flanders. "The Armada has arrived!" it said. He needed a quick reply.

21

Plymouth was in a fever. "The Armada is wonderful great and strong!" admitted Admiral Howard. Tomorrow it would arrive in the Channel: 130 ships, 11,000 sailors – and 19,000 soldiers trained to board and take English ships.

Now is the time to act!

On the night of 30th July, cleverly, in darkness, Admiral Howard led his ships out into Plymouth Sound. A decoy squadron created confusion. The main English fleet crossed ahead of the Armada... then sailed round till the wind was in their favour. At dawn, both fleets were in place.

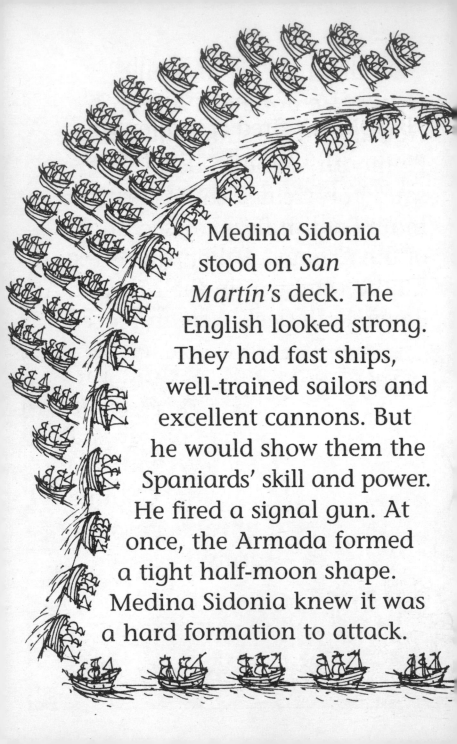

Medina Sidonia stood on *San Martín*'s deck. The English looked strong. They had fast ships, well-trained sailors and excellent cannons. But he would show them the Spaniards' skill and power. He fired a signal gun. At once, the Armada formed a tight half-moon shape. Medina Sidonia knew it was a hard formation to attack.

Suddenly, the little English barque *Disdain* sailed forward. "BOOM!" it fired a challenging shot... and the war had begun!

Lord Howard ordered a line of English ships to sail past the Spanish ships, firing from their sides, one after the other. Then they turned about and fired again.

But it was only a skirmish. Although the English came off best, the Armada sailed on – up the Channel, towards Parma's army.

LINE AHEAD ATTACK!

Medina Sidonia was worried. What should he do? There had been no reply from Parma. Was the army ready for them?

"I will sail on to Flanders," he resolved. "And if the English get close, our soldiers will grapple and board their ships. If they keep far off, then their guns will not harm us."

Unknown to Sidonia, Admiral Howard agreed. "All we can do now is give chase," he frowned. "Our ships are fast, and they sail well in the wind. But we need to close in to break the Armada's formation."

"BOOM!" A sudden blast shattered Spain's *San Salvador.* "ABANDON SHIP!" Medina Sidonia rescued the survivors – and its cargo of gold. They had to leave the ship to the English.

Close by, two
more Armada ships
collided, and the *Rosario*
lost a mast. Watchful on
the *Revenge*, Drake
attacked it at dawn. But
this slowed and broke up the
English fleet. The Spaniards
had time to recover. Frobisher
blamed Drake. "He kept by her
all night," he fumed,
"because he would
have the spoils." And
there *was* plenty of
gold for Drake...

At dawn on 2nd August, four small Spanish galleasses, with the wind behind them, suddenly closed in on Frobisher's mighty *Triumph*. Cannons roared...

The *Ark Royal* rushed in to help Frobisher. Then the wind changed, the ships moved apart, and another skirmish was over.

The Armada sailed on. England's ships followed, snapping at their heels.

There were other brief
tussles. Spanish soldiers strained
to jump on to English ships
when they strayed too
close. Howard was forced
to keep his ships back.

CLOSE IN!
GRAPPLE AND
BOARD!

STAY
CLEAR, USE
YOUR CANNONS!

His gunners fired round after
round... but did little harm. "We
will pluck their feathers by little
and little," Howard said grimly.
But both sides were running
low on ammunition, particularly
the Spanish...

On 6th August, the Armada reached Calais. No reply had come to Medina Sidonia's many messages to Parma in Flanders. "We cannot move far till Parma speaks," he fretted. "We must anchor and resupply here."

But, in the darkness, English ships lurked menacingly. "Prepare the hellships!" whispered Howard. At his words, brave crews sailed eight burning ships towards the Spanish fleet.

"FIRESHIPS!" Spanish watchmen panicked. "Cut your anchor ropes! RUN!"

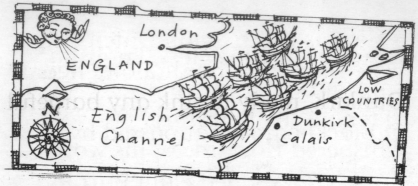

So the Armada scattered, and strong winds swept it east.

"No matter, it blows us nearer our Spanish army in Flanders," thought the Spanish commander.

But when we get there, how will we meet?

"If I sail into Dunkirk to fetch the army, we'll stick on the sandbanks. But Parma's barges can never reach open sea. The Dutch will pounce on them like cats."

He was right. Small Dutch ships were hiding in the shallows near Dunkirk, ready to sink any bargeful of Blackbeards that passed by.

So, Spain's invasion plan – its Enterprise on England – was in trouble. And now the fleets were at Gravelines. It was 8th August, and the wind was rising, buffeting the Armada as it lay close to the shore. Sidonia knew it could not go on.

We must fight here, close to our army in Flanders.

Now the English put a bold plan into action. Only firepower could destroy the Armada, Howard realised. "We'll get near them this time. Then we'll fire swiftly and often, and sink those Spanish galleons!"

"Fire on their seaward ships!" he yelled to his men. "Force their landward vessels to the shallows!"

Spanish and English ships sailed in close. Hull scraped on hull. An English sailor jumped on to a Spanish deck, and was instantly killed.

The English plan was working. "CRASH!" Shot struck the *San Martín*. Divers had to plug its holes. "BOOM!" Bullets rained down till the decks ran with blood. The *María Juan* sank.

The *San Mateo* is riddled with shot like a sieve!

In nine hours, the battle was done. "The Enterprise is over," said Captain Recalde. "We have hundreds of dead and many wounded," Medina Sidonia agreed. "Let us pray until dawn."

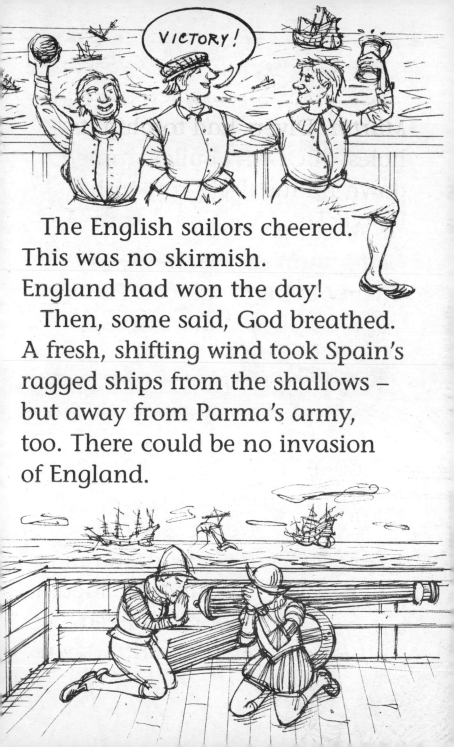

The English sailors cheered. This was no skirmish. England had won the day!

Then, some said, God breathed. A fresh, shifting wind took Spain's ragged ships from the shallows – but away from Parma's army, too. There could be no invasion of England.

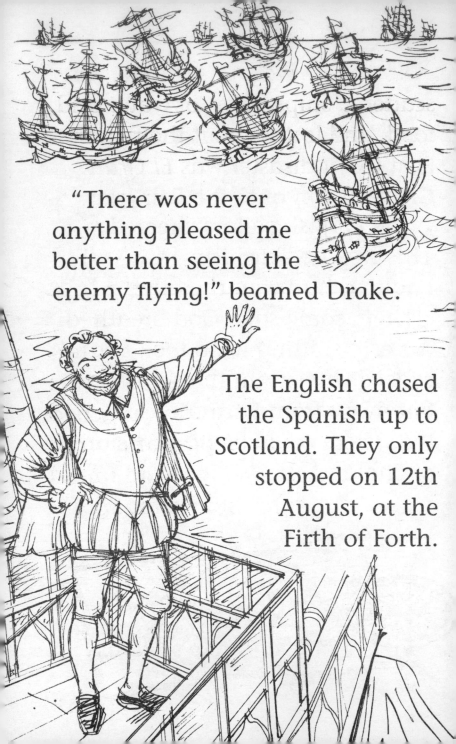

"There was never anything pleased me better than seeing the enemy flying!" beamed Drake.

The English chased the Spanish up to Scotland. They only stopped on 12th August, at the Firth of Forth.

Now there was no Armada. Just scattered ships, short of water and food, and lost without their charts. First to hit disaster was *El Gran Grifin*. It ran onto the Fair Isles.

A few survivors reached Scotland – not Spain's enemy – and found ships bound for Spain.

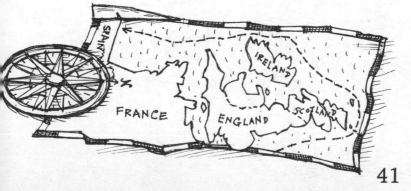

But storm followed storm. On Ireland's west coast, more Spanish ships were smashed on the rocks. The crew who made it to shore were robbed and a few killed.

Slowly, the Armada struggled back to Spain – only sixty ships made it. Forty-two had sunk and half the men had died. Medina Sidonia arrived on 21st September. "I am unable to describe to Your Majesty the misfortunes and miseries that have befallen us," he wrote in despair to his king.

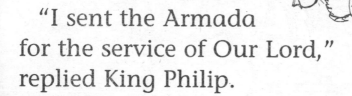

"I sent the Armada for the service of Our Lord," replied King Philip.

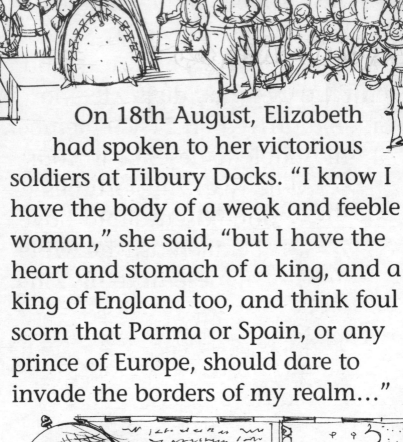

On 18th August, Elizabeth had spoken to her victorious soldiers at Tilbury Docks. "I know I have the body of a weak and feeble woman," she said, "but I have the heart and stomach of a king, and a king of England too, and think foul scorn that Parma or Spain, or any prince of Europe, should dare to invade the borders of my realm..."

England had won. In 1596 and 1597, Philip sent more Armadas. But they were failures, too. Spain's power, like its navy, could not match its rival England. Elizabeth's captains now sailed the world – for their Queen "Gloriana", and for England's trade, wealth and power!

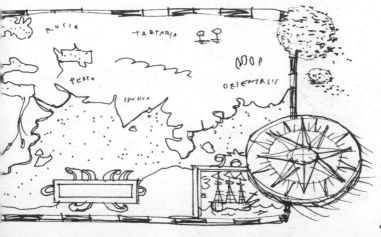

Timeline

1521   Spain conquers the Aztec Empire in Central America.

1534   Henry VIII and England break from the Roman Catholic Church.

1535   Spain conquers the Inca Empire in South America.

1556   Philip II becomes King of Spain and the Netherlands.

1558   Elizabeth becomes Queen of England.

1585   Drake attacks Spanish ships in Spanish America.
Elizabeth sends an army to help the Dutch fight the Spanish.

1586   Spain prepares to invade England.

1587   **February** Mary Queen of Scots is executed for her involvement in a Catholic plot against her cousin, Queen Elizabeth.
April Drake attacks Spanish ships in Cadiz.

1588   **May** Armada leaves Lisbon.
June England's fleet gathers in Plymouth.
21st July Armada sails for England.

46

25th July Sidonia sends his first message to Parma.

29th July Armada nears Cornwall. The English sail their ships from Plymouth into the English Channel.

30th – 31st July Armada enters the Channel and loses the *Rosario* and *San Salvador*.

2nd – 4th August English and Spanish ships fight off Portland Bill and the Isle of Wight.

6th August Armada reaches Calais.

7th – 8th August English fireships attack the anchored Armada.

8th August Final battle off Gravelines begins.

10th August Defeated Armada begins its return to Spain around Scotland and Ireland.

12th August English ships stop chasing the Armada.

18th August Elizabeth speaks to her soldiers and navy at Tilbury Docks.

From Mid-September Many Armada ships are wrecked.

20th September Sidonia arrives in Santander, Spain.

10th November King Philip of Spain says he wishes he was dead.

Glossary

Ammunition Bullets and shells, for example, that are fired from a weapon.

Barge A boat with a flat bottom used for carrying heavy loads.

Barque A sailing ship with three or more masts (poles that support the sails).

Blackbeards A nickname for members of the Spanish army.

Decoy Something used to lead people into a trap.

Galleasse A warship with three masts.

Galleon A large sailing ship with three or more masts used for war and trade.

Hellship A burning ship.

Low Countries The name given at the time to Belgium, Luxembourg and the Netherlands.

Privateer An armed ship working for, but not owned by, a government.

Skirmish A small battle.

Spymaster A person in charge of spies.

Squadron Part of one of the armed forces.